To The Chest... Support Group (see P.54)
All the best
from
Jean Sharaz
9/7/94

# IF NOT A MOTHER

Poems on infertility and childlessness

Compiled by Clare Butler

Published by Clare Butler, 72 Lynton Road, Chesham, Bucks

ISBN 0 952133 0 X

The poems by Jacqueline Brown are from *Thinking Egg*, published by Littlewood Arc, 1993.
'Cul-de-sac' by Simon Wrigley first appeared in *Spokes*, 1991.

Cover illustration: 'Who am I?' by Sandra Peaty.

Printed in the UK by The Print Centre, Chesham, Bucks

*CONTENTS*


Preface *John Dickson* 6
Introduction *Clare Butler* 7

*WHO AM I?* 9
If not a mother *Karen* 10
The distance between us *Jackie Head* 11
Primary infertility *Helen Dymond* 12
Borrowed grace *Cora Greenhill* 14
Extracts from *Thinking Egg* *Jacqueline Brown*
In the room (2) 15
Poaching 17
In the room (3) 18
Scrambled 20
Thinking egg 21

*REACHING OUT* 23
Prayer before conception *Meredith Wheeler* 24
Cold grey *Rosemary Crisp* 25
Learning to breathe *Jackie Head* 26
Wanting *Clare King* 27
Reaching out *Michelle Booth* 27
Slow spring *Jackie Head* 28

*EMPTY VESSEL ... BROKEN HEART* 31
Unbroken wall *Julie Owen* 32
Early November *Pearl Ray* 32
Deaf *Rosemary Crisp* 33
Expressions of a mother's guilt *M. Martin* 34
Forty-third spring *Cora Greenhill* 35
A quiet rage *Sandra Peaty* 36
One year on *Charlie Finch* 37
Is ever only this *Sharon Kelly* 38

Our first baby *Anne Hill* 39
On reflection *Anne Hill* 39
Petal child *Cora Greenhill* 40
Loss *Jennifer Hutchinson* 42
No visits today, please *Patricia* 43
Silence *Emma Laybourn* 44
Speaking hands *Sharon Kelly* 45
Empty *Lysanne Sizoo* 46
Names are not empty *Sharon Kelly* 47

*WOMEN'S WARD* 49
Women's ward *Judith Bolland* 50
Test tube baby *Annemarie Snodgrass* 51
Untitled *Angela Patchett* 52
Infertility (with endometriosis) *Alison Bailey* 53
Remembrance *Jean Sharaz* 54
Obsession *Gillian Bara* 56
Barren: infertile: childless *Chris Gothard* 57
Fruit *Judith Bolland* 59

*ON THE SIDELINE* 61
Sideline *Hilda Cotterill* 62
Sarah's song *Rowena White* 63
Poem *Michele* 64
Space invaders *Judy Kendall* 65
I, who have lost *Clare King* 66
No more *Julie Owen* 67
Do not tell me *Rosemary Crisp* 68
The luck of the draw *Julia Neville* 69

*MOVING ON* 71
Change *Rowena White* 72
Intestate *Eve Kenyon* 73
Moving on *Jackie Head* 74
Cul-de-sac *Simon Wrigley* 75
When I'm nursing a poem *Rowena White* 76
Small one *Chris Gothard* 77
Thought-child *Jackie Head* 78
Awards ceremony *Rowena White* 79
I am woman *Jackie Head* 80

Reflections on themes and issues *Gayle Letherby* 82

## *PREFACE*

Infertility, for most people who suffer, is a long drawn-out, painful and often damaging experience. So it should not be surprising that people reflect their feelings and situations by writing poetry.

ISSUE, the major charity working with infertile people, says that its role is to provide information and support and to represent the needs of the infertile to the rest of the population. Many people who join us see us as a source of information about the technicalities of treatment, where treatment might be found, and the cost that may have to be incurred. However, from our point of view, support for our members is far more important than information. The discovery of the inability to have children, whether because of your own problems, or of problems relating to your partner, or for no apparent reason, can be very difficult for some people to bear.

The role of poetry here is important because it is an attempt by human beings to get at their deepest emotions, to make sense of the experiences they are having. It has always been part of my own personal philosophy that however bad things are, at least if I can make sense of them, then they are of some value.

Poetry is a form of communication. Often for the writer it is an internal communication, an attempt to make contact with feelings and emotions, and to understand themselves in a way they can only do through this form of art. May I recommend this book to you.

*John Dickson*
Director, ISSUE

# *INTRODUCTION*

In mid-1992 I read a letter in the magazine of the infertility support organisation CHILD, describing one couple's six years of fertility problems culiminating in an ectopic pregnancy. It ended, '*How* do we face a childless future?' I wondered how many people there were facing the same anguish, worn down by emotional stress and the trauma of infertility treatment, feeling isolated from family, friends and society in general, their burden of grief unseen and unheard. I wanted them to have the opportunity to be heard. This book is the result.

I was astonished and delighted at the response to my requests for material – although saddened as well, since such a huge response to a few small advertisements must represent only a tiny proportion of the people affected. (Strangely, I received only one poem from a man.) There are poems from women who cannot conceive or whose partners cannot; who have miscarried or have had stillbirths; who have had a child but cannot have another. There are meticulously crafted reflections and violent outpourings of rage. There is pain and despair but also hope, love and humour. There are even some happy endings. I decided not to include information about the authors (which I often didn't have anyway), so I hope that the poems speak for themselves.

Compiling this book has been a great privilege. The credit for it is due not only to those whose contributions appear, but also to those who sent me items I regretfully had to decide to leave out, and to everyone who expressed interest in and encouragement for the project. Particular thanks go to Shannon Ford and Pam Berry for typing, and to Jackie Head for editorial wisdom. I am also grateful to The Open University for allowing me study leave to complete the work.

*Clare Butler*

Woman No. 1 *Sharon Kelly*

# WHO AM I?

This first section looks at the search for identity. For many women, the ability to have children is the definition of being female: the role of motherhood is at the core of their identity. This is more than a social and cultural construct: because we are animals, it is a biological urge; because we are human, it is a spiritual one. When 'life's longing for itself' is thwarted, the whole idea of self has to be reconstructed. We lose our connection with the future; we have to rethink our relationship to the past. And while the painful search for one's childless self can strengthen relationships with others, it can also destroy them.

## *IF NOT A MOTHER*

Who am I,
If not a mother?
My body feels different,
Lacking in hope, shrinking in acceptance.
Which road, if a choice, do I pursue?
Do I channel into what I do –
Neglecting the mother needing to be fulfilled?
Do I turn the mother on me, to nurture myself?
Do I become the career woman further, to compensate
  for not being a mother?
If not a mother, then what?

If not a mother, then maybe I don't want to be a wife,
If I'm not a mother, then I could be a lover to several.
Do I want a marriage when there's only ever two?
Do I make a home, a framework perfect to emphasise
  the gap of the two not being enough?
And does it mean that two not being enough is wrong,
  a fault in the relationship?
Do I express the creativity in making things, gardening,
  cooking?
Do I do other things that mothers don't do, like travel,
  indulgences, hobbies, therapy and self-improvement?
If not a mother, then what of my future?
Will anyone visit me when I am old?
Who will remember me, my birthdays,
If my partner/husband/lover dies?
If not a mother, then who *will* I be now,
If this part of me is unexpressed?
Who am I, what am I instead?

*Karen*

## *THE DISTANCE BETWEEN US*

The distance between us
is sometimes so small
sometimes a gaping chasm
of mismatched emotions.
I want everything to be all right
and everything to be right
between us.
You a childless father
I a barren mother
have so little to draw us
out of ourselves
that in the wasted moments
such as this,
I wonder if we will ever
turn this dumb agony
into spoken grief,
or whether its intensity
will break us
and leave us
with only distance between us.

*Jackie Head*

## *PRIMARY INFERTILITY*

so you want a song of infertility
you want to know how old Sarah felt
before the angel forgave her with Isaac
for what she hadn't done
    don't ask said he,
    what's forty years of pain?
    you are all God's children

the sow with her eighteen teats
kneedeep in shit, rope-throated for the butcher's knife can still
smile on her captors
as the teats
are eighteen ways caressed
the world waits
to eat her mammaries at the Sabbath feast
but first
she has reincarnated gammon and grunting
for the universe

balls said the angel
ludicrous conceit
do you want your legs spread and your guts
pulled from you as a living head?
Worry    Guilt    Potty
training teenage dropout drugs no gratitude

Woman of the new millenium
veil yourself
in friendship sex career
be a man if you will
get therapy adopt a Romanian
there are far, he cried
too many children in the world

what am I then
since my body
has failed to repay?

just, as Lawrence softly said of Connie Chatterly,
a thing of terrors
humiliation worse, far worse
than immorality

there are sisters who exercise choice but I
    am not one
the womb has me in thrall
to its useless bloat and vomit
as the moon darkens my room
    ovaries lie in brain like unpicked fruit
        even in sleep
            imploding

I want to kill the child within me
how do you mothers
feel about that?

*Helen Dymond*

## *BORROWED GRACE*

Clumsy in snorkel, and flippers
that drag on the sand until I'm afloat
when breasts and belly hang weightless:
the water lending grace that's not our own

to our white bodies floating like distorted moons
through liquid skies deepening from radiant blue
through twilight jade to indigo
as the sea-bed shelves suddenly.

I watch an octopus shift under its stone,
puff sand, twitch a tentacle,
then drift to where the ocean has no floor
and the clear darkness is alight

with multitudes of gold-green, nib-sized fish.
Somewhere down there I suspend my disbelief
accept the infinite mystery of the deep
written on white tampons, unstained as the moon turned:

somewhere in me was a sea
large enough for a shoal to swim in
a sea-bed safe enough to sink in
send out tentacles and feed.

*Cora Greenhill*

FROM *THINKING EGG*

## *IN THE ROOM (2)*

On but paper sheeting
a woman is lying
on her side, knees to nose
like an ovenready chicken

another woman is stroking
her hand clenched till skin
feels close to tearing, like
she's a baby like she's a child

*Just relax if you can*
*Clever girl      that's right*

a man in a clean white coat's
an invisible voice moving
unseen in the greenpaint room
just a paper rustle, a mumble

she is not a clever girl
she is not a good girl
the snap of the rubber glove
condemns; the blue paper rucks
with her guilt

under a rubber membrane fingers
inquire, tamper – slick fingers
with no face eyes colour hair –
she has unbodied his fingers

*Try to relax      it'll hurt less*

a woman is severing a body into bits
guillotine snaps and the head floats
free, snap and snap through the pubic
bone and the body rises, next the legs;
on the blue paper sheet is a tiny pocket
of air encased in stoneskin and a wet
finger learning something and a mind
recording      determined to forget

the other woman is helping her from the bed
saying *It's all right, it's all over,*
saying *There, dear* ... but the silly eyes
can't not look at the map of Africa
damp-etched on the blue paper sheeting
can't not fast forward to all the miles
and miles to go... desert and sea
and desert and sea before the ghost
of a landing

## *POACHING*

She has heard the women whispering
in hospital rooms of suffering,
pain, blood.

She has stood palefaced in the margins
looking and listening, separate
from them.

while they slept, she has walked in her head
through the bluelit quiet ward, skirting
the nurse,

toe-stepped along the white corridor,
keeping to walls, to where milky kids
snuffle;

she's walked further to a flurried place
where infants lie flat under glass, taped
to tubes.

Sleepwalking, she has understood theft,
the urge to prise open, steal and hide,
not care

that another woman is crying somewhere
just so long as her own boat of arms
is full.

## *IN THE ROOM (3)*

In the dayroom the woman is sitting,
back to the TV, watching the wall.
The woman's body is rocking
forward back, forward back,
ticktock ticktock.
Fragments of song
dribble from her mouth.
If anyone were listening
they'd hear *chicken egg baby* then
half-audible runs of wordless tune.

No-one is listening.

If the woman were to turn
anyone watching would see
how each cupped palm cradles an elbow
holds it still against the body's motion.
Anyone looking would see a stone oval
where the face should be, two blobs
of blue glass at its widest point.

No-one is looking.

If Stoneface were to rotate
from yellow wall to direct light
the blue glass blobs would see spring
framed in the window – a green lawn
spattered with dandelions,
a horsechestnut bursting,
a sky brailled with birds.

She will not turn.

If anyone were recording the scene
nothing would happen –
back-view of a to–fro rocking woman,
tiny clutches of song
pan-out to yellow walls
a yolk-spattered lawn
pan-in to a black and white TV.

No-one is recording,

No-one has the technology
to record the clackclack
of a mind speedshuttling
woof across frayed warp
weaving what may turn out to be
a cradle-cloth or winding sheet,

no-one knows.

## *SCRAMBLED*

it's dark    don't like the dark
sing a song make the dark go away
*look what they've done to my song, Ma*
*lalalalalalala* must've done wrong
bad egg    cracked egg    smacksmacksmack
poor egg    poor hen    Humpty Dumpty Dad
in bits and pieces all the King's horses
and all the King's men can't put Humpty
together again    "puir wee hen" says Humpty
when baby stumbles and tumbles    when the bough
breaks    puir wee hen when when will you lay
me an egg for my tea? Not a stone egg    Silly
hen    Bad hen    smacksmack    sticks and stones
will break my bones    chop off her head.
The blood's all red
*look what they've done to my brain, Ma*
*they've picked it like a chicken-bone*
*and* chickchickchickchick chicken    Run quick
cradle's falling Ma    catch Baby Bunting
fetch Daddy    Daddy's gone a hunting somebody
catch her too late    can't put her together
again    say something
Bye Baby Bunting    bye baby    baby doesn't
like the dark    sing song make dark go away

## *THINKING EGG*

In the warm kitchen
two women are sitting
confiding failings, fears.
One woman is me.

… *like an egg* I'm saying
*one minute tough enough*
*to withstand anything, next*
*a fingertip could crack me* …

The other woman is literal –
she'll have no truck with metaphor
*No*      she's saying      *No you are not*
an egg      You are a woman

and yes, my literal friend,
I guess you are right,
but I'm a woman thinking egg
and staggering under its weight.

*Jacqueline Brown*

Borne *Sharon Kelly*

# REACHING OUT

This section is about longing and hope. The longing of unfulfilled love can be overwhelming. If you are trying to have a baby, every month that tiny seed of hope which refuses to die is shattered once again. Given month after month, year after year of disappointment, it is remarkable that those trying to conceive go on hoping. But they do.

## *PRAYER BEFORE CONCEPTION*

Let your womb be moist in the velvet darkness.
Cradle me with gentle ease.
Send from your heart a silver cord
Flowing with tender love and empathy,
Binding me to you.
Gather round the pure colours of the rainbow
For my suchness is built of this.

Let the moment of my birth arrive in its own right season.
Be calm and patient.
Let father draw near to steady us through the journey,
A dark tunnel, then the light.

And in that starburst moment
When my eyes first open,
Let the lights be soft, the sounds low.
Lay me on your breast,
Where I can rest to the lullaby of your heartbeat.

*Meredith Wheeler*

## *COLD GREY*

I was foolish
To look down
That shaft of light,
I mistakenly took
As the future.
The pastel shades of my dreams
So clear then
As I thought.
Somehow
The brightness dimmed.
My world sank
In to a cold grey.

*Rosemary Crisp*

## *LEARNING TO BREATHE*

Sometimes
I have
such longings
for a child,
I cannot breathe
properly,
or think
properly.
Something tells me
it would be
easier,
if I could not
breathe
or think
at all.
Then at least
I would not
splutter out my life
in unfulfilled
half-breaths
gasping for thought.

*Jackie Head*

## *WANTING*

How can you grieve
For that which you never had?
I feel bereft, and alone
Yet am no different to before
– Before I began trying
To create you.
My monthly blues
Are not from an aching back
But from an aching heart.
I long for the day
I can hold you,
When I can touch you
And say "This is my child."

*Clare King*

## *REACHING OUT*

Was that a child's cry
That disturbed my sleep?
Or has desparate yearning
Gone too deep?
Realisation awakes with the dawn,
The silence oppresses,
Consumes the morn.
There is no child here,
Nor ever will be.
The plea that was uttered
Came from me.

*Michelle Booth*

## *SLOW SPRING*

This year the spring seems muted.
This isn't just my idea,
many have noticed it.
A cold winter would have brought spring in a flourish,
the warmth and ease we have had
has made softer, less defined changes.
For me this is the greatest blessing,
A normal spring,
its blossoms full and heavy,
its flowers pregnant
with new life,
would have broken me.
As it is the spring has suited my own mood.

There are traces of new life,
but with it come the sadnesses
of magnolias half open,
and cherry trees
frail and vulnerable
in their moves to summer.

It is as though the gentle life force
is edging me forward.
My own life forces
encourage me to new growth
and open
a tender well of hopefulness.

I am the spring blossom
daring to lead a path
towards a future.
I am the silent
breaking of bluebells
into an unfamiliar new sphere.

My own petals
open slowly,
so much so that I don't see the change
as clearly as others
watching the delicate steps I am taking.
There are longer breaks of happiness
between the shattering bouts of depression.
I do more,
I plan an uncertain walk to recovery.
The slow spring guides me on
and I am grateful for its nudging moves
towards a summer
that will come.

*Jackie Head*

Miscarry III *Sharon Kelly*

# EMPTY VESSEL ... BROKEN HEART

Anyone who has tried to conceive and failed, or who has lost a child, knows of times when it feels as if the spirit has reached rock bottom. Anguish – grief – rage – guilt – despair. These are our responses to loss: loss of the child who dies in the womb or at birth; loss of the child who cannot be conceived but who is no less real in our imagination and in our heart; loss of our self constructed in relation to that child. We are powerless against Nature. The emptiness can be papered over – but can it ever be mended, filled?
Perhaps the only comfort in this deepest sorrow is to find words that capture the emotions and so give the broken heart a voice.

## *UNBROKEN WALL*

The pain does not go away,
it's there inside you every day.

It lies dormant, waiting for a chance to break
to bring you to your knees with pain
and flowing tears and empty heart like rock,
not heavy but still, solid and strangely hollow
and then once more you build up the wall
and file away the pain.

It does not go away,
it's there inside you each and every day.

*Julie Owen*

## *EARLY NOVEMBER*

Loneliness, when will you be done with me?
I have not sought you, yet every time
I think I have all I need,
There you are again.

Spare me now this shedding of tears,
This cold beauty, frost on the pond.
You have had my childhood, must you take
My motherhood also?

*Pearl Ray*

## *DEAF*

Conscious all the time
Of her ever-increasing
Bulging belly
I scream so loud
Inside my skull
That I make myself deaf.

Deaf to reason
Deaf to finding solace
In other things.
Deaf to reasonable distractions
That take me away
From that gnawing pain.
More a dull ache
An emptiness.
A refusal of acceptance
That tries to crowd in,
Muscle its way
To the centre of my brain.

*Rosemary Crisp*

## *EXPRESSIONS OF A MOTHER'S GUILT*

The searing pain inside,
The day you said goodbye;
You left me without warning;
Left me with only tears to cry.

No more than just a planted seed –
You had so much time to grow.
But Fate just had to stamp his feet
And you, I never got to know.

Alone and without you,
I tried to carry on;
But oh, so hard to understand
The fact that you were gone.

I couldn't tell a soul –
No-one's heart must I break.
I alone must bear the cost
Of putting so much at stake.

Your father never knew,
He wouldn't have stayed for long.
But please forgive your mother
For whatever she did wrong.

Today you would have been here,
the 24th of June.
Instead, you're somewhere out of reach
Beyond the sun, the stars, the moon.

*M. Martin*

## *FORTY-THIRD SPRING*

Frantic with air freight, the usual morning
fizzes with bird busy-ness
birth business

Overdue rain in the night stained the deep soil
rootlings can stretch and drink
seed leaves uncurl

Relentless the blood aches from my shrinking womb
thrums on the slackening drum
skin sagging dully

Dark clouds still hang like a hen
on this cold clutch of spring.
Day 29. Unhatched. Infertile.

*Cora Greenhill*

## *A QUIET RAGE*

Thirty-five days – a little unusual
The fantasies begin.
Breaking the news.
May will be the month,
A blossoming time of new growth.

This is foolish,
I tell nobody
Spare myself the embarrassment
The explanation.

And so to bed
Another day gone
This is unusual.
Could this be ‘it’?
Don’t panic, I say
Smothering the excitement

I beg the fantasies to stop.

Final pee
And there it is
Of course it is
Sharp back ache an hour ago
And now …

Grasping hold of a steel cord within
No tears are allowed to come.
Feeling weary and cheated
Turning in on myself,
I rage quietly
Damn it, damn it all.
Why us?

*Sandra Peaty*

## *ONE YEAR ON*

If I let go, there will be a
Cascade, an
Almighty avalanche;
I will weep until the sun dawns
    until there are no more tears left in the world
    until my whole being rots away.

My arms hang limp at my side.
I sit on the floor, unable to move,
I can reach no lower.

*Charlie Finch*

## *IS EVER ONLY THIS*

There is a dark part
to his eye,
unspeakable
and arms crossed in resignation.

Is ever only this
– this stillness,
as rests my fallen hair.

There is ever only this.
Immeasurable distance,
these tears fall to it.

to the conclusion.
All things considered
– How quietly he stood
on the edge of mystery,
watching and involved.

Somewhere someone waited.
This little peace,
this wide farewell.

*Sharon Kelly*

## *OUR FIRST BABY*

Although we never knew you
Although we never saw you
With all our hearts we loved you
All the same.

*Anne Hill*

## *ON REFLECTION*

If I had a spirit, it's broken
If I had a heart, it's torn in two
If I had a dream, it's shattered
If I had a smile, it's subdued.

*Anne Hill*

## *PETAL CHILD*

There is no way
there is no right way
we have not been taught
any way of being with this
we have no hammock of belief to lie back in
no sustaining truth
to feed us in this wilderness of loss

we have no rites passed down
for your passing on
can only listen to what our hearts invent
allow all our hearts to invent
from their love and grief
each in our own way for all of us

but after the days of womanly waiting
the still ache of unknowing
the suspension of active life
in the blank ignorance of daylight
while inside life and death
held silent conference

and after my night of untimely labour
when the body decreed
I must use my ancient knowledge
of birth breathing
against the painful spasms
that leave no room for doubt

when I have no choice but to co-operate
in freeing you
from the greedy embrace of my flesh
our flesh
our shared genetic stock
life's playtime from eternity

you linger awhile in the ether
are dandled in my trance of love
dancing with your company of souls
one new petal brighter than the many
shining your goodbye
waving God by me
to comfort me
you comfort me
oh my daughter.

*Cora Greenhill*

## *LOSS*

Pain, unseen yet deep.
Gnawing sorrow of the heart
Unnoticed even by those closest to me,
Surprisingly.
Pain hidden perhaps too well.

Searing sense of loss
Tears my heart apart again.
Ancient wounds prised open ruthlessly
By one word, one glimpse too many
Of newborn babes in loving arms,
While my empty arms ache.

What should have been
Now will not be –
My long-awaited baby gone
Before we had a chance to meet.
Gone to eternity before me,
Waiting there for me,
While I am here
Yearning for her.
But knowing that, one day
She and I will meet …

*Jennifer Hutchinson*

## *NO VISITS TODAY, PLEASE*

No visits today, please.
We don't want you flaunting your children and fertility here.

Can't you see my grief?
No matter how you want to help, you can't.
You can't put me right, no-one can
But me.

I want time to think,
To mill this feeling around my head until it's all ground out.
It never seems to end,
This feeling.

So leave me alone, drowning in my own self-pity.
I don't want to pretend with you that I'm all right,
Because I'm not.
And probably won't be until that something you take for granted
Happens to *me*.

*Patricia*

*SILENCE*

"Be generous," she says,
Slumped in the flotsam of her family.
"Enjoy what's here:
Rejoice in what you have." I try,
But silence cannot cheer.

"You're fortunate," she says,
As doors bang, voices shout and plead,
Complain and curse:
"You'll never have all this." Indeed,
But silence thinks there's worse.

"So tedious!" she says,
"The selfsame query twenty times,
The precious hoard
Of dreadful jokes, the litany of rhymes."
But silence is not bored.

"And patience, too," she says,
"With streams of babbling words to trawl
And slowly sift
For meaning, how days begin to crawl."
But silence says, Too swift.

"No sleepless nights," she says,
"No wails to wake you with a start,
No red-rimmed eyes."
She's wrong. It's in the night's sad heart
That silence cries.

*Emma Laybourn*

## *SPEAKING HANDS*

I see your
speaking hands fall
empty. Silence
where I bore him.

Oblivious now to
the comfort of hands,
preciously nursed
like the unhealing sick.

No longer whole,
my parts lie like scraps
beside me. The severed
womb to tin bowls,
you to God.

*Sharon Kelly*

## *EMPTY*

I feel barren, hollow,
my belly an empty vessel under a broken heart.
Where once was life
echo the anguished cries
of a soul torn apart.

My hand rests there, where *you* should have been,
and a silent tear muffles an angry scream.

Outside, Nature rejuvenates once more,
with the sickening ease
of a talented whore.

Where once was joy,
suspicion now reigns.
Whatever happens,
I won't trust again.

Who was to say, why me,
why not me?
If only I knew
what the future would be.

*Lysanne Sizoo*

## *NAMES ARE NOT EMPTY*

You said it was too late
for names,
two hearts in your hand.
It was then your grief became tears.

You said goodbye to your
two mid-fielders.
Seems no rules to
the game; this
random risk of
catastrophe.

Now you'll craft a cradle box,
mending your pitch.
A father's hand.
The natural order
rocking and swaying.

*Sharon Kelly*

Woman No. 4 *Sharon Kelly*

# WOMEN'S WARD

Advances in medical science have meant that many more women who might otherwise have remained childless have been able to have children. But reproductive technology has a downside – the clinic or ward, focused on the technological, sometimes at the expense of the human, is the stuff nightmares are made of. Not being able to bear a child is humiliating and stressful enough to start with. If you're lucky enough to find treatment locally, the fertility clinic may be part of the antenatal clinic. You may be seen by a male gynaecologist with no specialist knowledge of infertility, who treats you with as much concern as if you had an ingrowing toenail. If you need hospital treatment, you may well find yourself in the next bed to somebody having an abortion (a situation distressing to both women). And while for some the hope held out by high-tech treatment – if they can afford it – is justified, those magazine articles about 'miracle babies' don't often mention that the majority of couples go through it all for nothing.

## *WOMEN'S WARD*

1
A tacit silence on this ward.
For you, the words are clinical,
Biblical. A scar crooks
on your belly. Each month
you bleed, emptying.

Used to the press
of the stirrups at the back of your knees –
the speculum, steel, cold tile – you bless
the casual kindness of nurses.

2
You meet me with your quick
crabwise shuffle. I've brought
forced hothouse narcissi, still
lipped in their pale hoods.

You ask me to wash your hair.
We perch on the edge
of the stained enamel bath – I'm clumsy,
feel that everywhere I touch
is tender – but you grin, "Rub harder".

I lather and rinse your dark
bent head, covering the veiled
swell of your skull: as close then
as I'll ever come.

*Judith Bolland*

## *TEST TUBE BABY*

There! A heap of broken dreams
cascades down deep into
a soul swollen with hope.
An orange rose screams to
skies drenched with rain.
Divide! I cried in the
night, etherised, numbed,
to the copper beeches
nodding to the fern-winged stream.
They flew a kite
yellow and red with satin
bands in baby-colours.
And there! unknown,
uncanny in a dish
smooth with silky fluid,
the doctors' secret,
the promise of wonder
it was, shedding its
genes, dividing,
two into four,
four into eight,
forever, we hoped.
But hubris it is
to coax out Nature's
most subtle secrets:
too many dreams fall prey
to her unfathomable ways.

*Annemarie Snodgrass*

*UNTITLED*

The tests proved your infertility,
and the doctor's words hung
over us both,
descending
threatening to envelop us
in their gloom.
Inside I screamed
why us?
We loved children,
could give them so much,
but we would never know
that joy,
and were to be denied
the experience of childbirth,
of giving life to our seed.
For him the test proved
so much more.
His place in the world
as a man
had been thrown to the test.
He felt inadequate,
and I knew I must hide my despair,
his burden was great enough
without having to carry mine too.
When we had met
so long ago,
I knew he would be the father
of four lovely children,
but now there would be none.
The doctor was cold, insensitive
to our pain,
we were just one of the couples
he had to see on that day.

As we left his office
my heavy heart broke,
as the first thing I saw
was a child,
the child I knew now
could never be mine.

*Angela Patchett*

## *INFERTILITY (WITH ENDOMETRIOSIS)*

The interminable agony
Dulls occasionally into pain,
Silently, violently
it stabs,
Slithering through your guts.

A tube provides …
futile hopes
An impossible child
Your release.

Life passes by
You writhe –
    occasionally –
    with pain.

Make your choice.
    which alternative?
There is no real decision
    – just suffering.

*Alison Bailey*

## *REMEMBRANCE*

Little baby, I dreamt of you
As I bore the injections and the pain,
The probing of my body
Again and again.
Little baby, I dreamt of you
As I lay in my hospital bed
After all the eggs had been taken out from my ovaries
And transported to the laboratory.
Little baby, I saw you in the lab
Under the microscope
When you were just a three-day-old embryo.
We looked and wondered
Will you be a boy or a girl
Before you are transported back into my womb?
You should have seen the beam of pride
Upon your Daddy's face!
Oh, that you had looked and seen
The look of wonder on my face!
My wide-eyed amazement!
How our two adopted children
So looked forward to your birth!
We talked about the names you'd have
Laughed at my increasing girth!
Oh, how we loved those positive pregnancy tests!
The scans that showed you growing in my womb.
But then at ten weeks, the shock upon the doctor's face –
"Your baby's gone, just an embryonic sac in its place."
Where did you go?
Oh, the feeling of being still pregnant
As I lay on that hospital bed!
A shot of anaesthetic
My womb is scraped of all evidence of conception.
I wake up with an empty womb
I cry.

The nurses cannot understand the reason why I cry
They see miscarriages every day
It's nothing new to them.
Home I go to the comfort of my family.
"Where did the baby go?" my children ask.
I try to explain, through the pain
And weep again.
For weeks I still think of you:
Where did you go, my baby dear?
What was in the world you feared?
Here lies an empty cradle,
An empty heart,
An empty womb.
Are you dancing with angels now?
I wonder, should we try again?
Go through the pain
Again?

*Jean Sharaz*

*OBSESSION*

In the waiting room,
we sit amongst women
whose fertility hangs off them;
their bellies are ripe melons
ready for the harvest.
I am a fruit that has had
all its juice sucked out –
a discarded skin.

In the consultation room,
they discuss the statistics.
"You're not on your own.
There may be nothing wrong,
except for stress. Relax.
We'll run some tests.
Have sex at least every other day
but, *don't* become obsessed."

We head for the exit
and have to pass Mothercare.
It opens its doors to those
who breed successfully.
I spy, with my little eye …
(I play the game without you)
abacus, babygro, carrycot – STOP!
Remember, *don't* become obsessed.

*Gillian Bara*

## *BARREN: INFERTILE: CHILDLESS*

I

BARREN: INFERTILE: CHILDLESS
the names they wouldn't say
labels I gave myself
definitions of this lack.
I am less, reduced by this
unwomanly, abnormal.

"I'm sorry to tell you that it's extremely unlikely
you'll ever have a child."
"Quite a mess in there: can't see how it would be possible."
This said not looking at me: read from notes,
thrown off over a male shoulder,
For all to hear
And witness my public shame, my utter humiliation
My empty, empty womb
My failure.
All while I'm still sore and bleeding – physically and
  emotionally
From yet another (the last?) operation
To try and discover WHY.

They had given up. I was abandoned to the grey, flat,
Second-best future of the childless.

"Best turn your mind to something else, my dear/
Get yourself a job/ Go on holiday/
Perhaps it was meant to be" (delete cliché as appropriate).

*God!* I could rip through, SCREAM at their clichés,
Their not wanting to know
Not wanting to see the pain.
And their guilt at their own inadequacy or good fortune.

II

'They' were wrong, weren't they, small one?
'They' say they have no idea how you came about
How, unlike all the others, you then insisted on staying
On waiting the full, long, ripe months
To be born.

I know why. I know how.
Because I *would not* give up hope
Because I was *so* determined
Because I prayed to something even more than
Our traditional, so-male God,
Something fecund, primeval, the Mother of the Earth,
The original Goddess.
And because one night, I dreamt of you,
Looking just as you do now,
Knowing you were waiting to come to me.

And you are here – two of you now.
And I have come out of the void, my wilderness
Into the light and fertile place
Here with you both.

*Chris Gothard*

## *FRUIT*

Your garden seems wilder this year.
I find you pulling fruit, palms
streaked with berry blood.

In the kitchen we breathe yeast, the house
is heavy with it; pulp
in an earthenware bowl seeps
through its muslin caul.

You repeat the news quietly – the phrase,
secondary infertility, clipped,
already practised.

Strange, you say, lying prone
in the dark room while they searched
for defects on the screen – cloudy
monochrome windings, flutterings.
You saw yourself exposed, negative.

I watch your measured movements;
you stir the must, weigh sugar,
add nutrient, lemons,
checking for astringency,
cover the crock closely.

Later we share last year's harvest; wine
the colour of a wound, deepening.

*Judith Bolland*

Woman No. 7 *Sharon Kelly*

# ON THE SIDELINE

Our society does not embrace the childless woman, whether or not she is childless by choice. From an early age she is likely to have internalised the belief that motherhood is at least part of her role in life and her route to ultimate fulfilment. She has few alternative role models. By the time she reaches her thirties she will probably not have many childless friends or colleagues. She is apt to be regarded with suspicion and even hostility. Those who know about her situation are inclined to make a joke of it, to tell her she's lucky, to offer to lend her their children, to tell her that children aren't everything, to dismiss it with 'never mind, you can always adopt'. Women have the right to choose – but some don't have the chance.

## *SIDELINE*

Sitting outside
This huddle of women,
She hears
Of epidural,
Caesarian,
Forceps,
And the breaking of waters.

She has no part
Of this their ultimate.
"It was difficult."
"I thought I'd die."
"You forget, of course."
"So wonderful,
Afterwards."

She listens, bemused,
Feels her unwrenched body
Inviolate.

She retreats
From their orgy
Of blood and torn tissue.
Her mind splits
Between envy and pity.

She is not sure
She has known no division of herself.
Witholds,
Is withheld,
On the sideline.

*Hilda Cotterill*

## *SARAH'S SONG*

Why do you tell them I'm your sister?
Are you so ashamed to own a barren wife
You pass me off, albeit to kings,
As an available all-purpose concubine,
Having no status being empty.
And yet I am still lovely,
Your covert intimacies tell me so
And we have journeyed far
Through the wilderness with hope,
Have seen the secret well-springs,
How the asses feed, the desert flowers.
I wish that I could help you,
I wish I knew why God witholds blessing.
But let me hold you nonetheless
And comfort you and maybe, just maybe
We will dream a child.

(Reference is Genesis Ch.11 when Abraham, the rat, afraid that the foreign kings would kill him for Sarah, his beautiful but barren wife, pretended she was his sister.)

*Rowena White*

*POEM*

I stroke my barren stomach,
Aching with emptiness;
Whilst all around me,
Friends and family
Announce their news.
And I smile
And force congratulations
Out of my burning throat.
Unshed tears sting my eyes,
And guilt for feeling this way
Burdens my head and heart.
People tell me to be patient;
That my time will come.
And I try so hard,
Throw myself into other things.
I cling on to my hopes and dreams,
Which are all I have,
And then the GP tries
To destroy even these
With her careless words,
As she glances at the photos
Of her babies, on the desk.
And I want to grab her,
To shake her,
And beg her to help.
But instead I smile,
Clench my fists,
Fight back the tears,
And try to carry on.

*Michele*

*SPACE INVADERS*

they call it

Baby sprouting country

the air is ripe with it
greedily sucking out the life
torn from complaisant wombs

Easy as guilt
they say
natural as breathing

little buggers
they never ask our opinion

We invite You
        to
A Hot Night's Reproductive Sex
(The Fruits of Passion)

and they creep darkly past
crumbled defences
lust dissembling love

Once planted the idea roots in
like a mounded grave to shroud the schooled anxiety

yet swelling or flat we remain
the container
the un-consulted

*Judy Kendall*

## *I, WHO HAVE LOST*

Why do they have to put me here
In this insanity?
I, who have lost,
I, who have never had,
Amongst these happy women
With their bundles of joy.
Right now,
I would rather be in jail
Or hell,
For nothing can be as bad
As this intolerable happiness
Of new motherhood.

*Clare King*

## *NO MORE*

I can't take any more of the mental
strain or the emotional pain.
I'm empty, I'm hollow, there is nothing inside.

Just a front with a laugh and a smile but I'm here inside
crying for help, but no-one notices.
WHY?

No-one sees because they can't cope
with this pain I'm in, have seen and felt.
No-one wants to talk about it,
hush not a word about it.

WHY NOT?
I need to talk and I need someone to listen.

Only my husband, so strong he is
to listen to my sobbing tears
through the years and yet more years to come.

Through future years I'll weep
but we have each other at least.

*Julie Owen*

## *DO NOT TELL ME*

Do not tell me
It does not hurt
When you hear another
One of those
Ten green bottles has fallen.

Do not tell me
It does not grip
At your throat
To watch her waist expanding
Day after day, week after week.

You grit your teeth
Until they splinter in your head
When she tells you
That the nine months
Is taking a long time.

So does Eternity
You say under your breath.
The pain oozing
Through every pore,
But not showing on your face.

*Rosemary Crisp*

## *THE LUCK OF THE DRAW*

Have you heard Catherine's splendid news?
She says, catching the sharpness of bile in her throat,
smoothing her voice over the trap of the telephone line,
honing the edge of the pain.

Due in August, Catherine told me.
She says, checking her smile in the mirror,
watching the practised laughter lines at the edge of her
  eyes,
and the brave slant of her lips.

Booked at Queen Charlotte's? I'm not surprised.
She says, glimpsing her shadow on the wall,
belly curved by the evening sun,
mocking the hollow within.

The doctors there are very good.
She says, feeling her thighs tense and contract,
mindful of all the exploratory testing
of fruitless indignity.

Yes, quite a change in their lives, I'm sure.
She closes the conversation, cuts off the phone,
cradling emptiness in the crook of her arm
and a void in her heart.

*Julia Neville*

Woman No. 6 *Sharon Kelly*

# MOVING ON

Involuntary childlessness is a bereavement, but the grief cannot be focused on a single event to 'get over' or 'come to terms with'. Some people may feel trapped in it for ever; others may find ways towards a resolution, an alternative, an answer to the question 'who am I … if not a mother?'

## *CHANGE*

A sense of loss
But losing something that was hardly there
Or seldom thought about, at least.
Now letting go without the option.
All those dreams of empty rooms and something
Missing, searching through to find, I knew not what,
Come home to me.

Like seeing something in the corner of my eye,
Occasionally the tides turn as they used;
I see the child flit round a corner
Just before I reach the place,
You who I never carried, never laboured
To produce, you haunt the edge of dreaming
Like the dead sister I can just remember
But can't be sure the memory is mine …

My mother gave me an old ottoman,
A bedding chest that had been hers
and when I cleaned it out, I found beneath the lining
An envelope – a broken candle and first-birthday cards,
All she had kept of the dead child.
I didn't have the nerve to give them back,
Admit I knew. I kept her secret.

And I peek nervously at odd occasions
When I might have answered yes to faint
Maternal echoes, allowed to come to birth
The waiting child and stifled down instead
The woman who craved life as much
And took a forty-year gestation to emerge
Full-grown, triumphant, from my seething brain.

Child, I denied you several times
And now I hear your intermittent laughter
Even further down the garden, catch
The merest glimpse of your bright hair
Around the corners of the hedges.
If I called now, could you still hear me?

*Rowena White*

## *INTESTATE*

No seed of mine will walk this earth,
I'll leave no sign of any worth,
Materially.

The earth will turn upon its course,
The stars will burn, there'll be no pause
Eternally.

And none shall know I've ever been,
The spinning years will change the scene
Remorselessly.

But yet I hope, enduring still,
My thoughts and dreams forever will
Live after me.

*Eve Kenyon (1924–1991)*

## *MOVING ON*

I have made a clay model
of the dove of peace.
It is for my parents who understand much
of my deep grief
my deep yearning.
It is right that they should have such peace.

I remember, before,
watching them
and noticing their forgetfulness.
Now I notice the difference less and less,
because I too leave pencils and letters
in irretrievable black holes of memory.

Tonight I painted a picture for our bedroom
and called it 'Spring',
but I feel that it too is for
my parents,
who know the joys and sorrows
of the changing seasons
in their own lives.

*Jackie Head*

## *CUL-DE-SAC*

We live at the end of a cul-de-sac
And, until life slowly realised the metaphor,
That just meant a more open aspect –
Now soon to be closed by a housing estate, and,
Ironically, the disfigurement of the cul-de-sac.

We can still look out over the field
Where the hectic wind inflames our trawling thorn
Which bursts fitfully with blooming plastic
(Our hedge chokes with terminal litter)
Caught like so many mad flowers in its throat.

The furrows run away from the house
And menstrually disappear in a green labour,
Contrasting oddly with the red and childless house
In which we count the days of our confinement,
Conscious of how inwardly things have turned out.

Our cul-de-sac is one of two parallel roads
Which will become a crescent when *developed* –
Whose metaphorical translation makes us laugh
To think that by the time the field is cropped brick red
We will have literally grown out of this.

*Simon Wrigley*

## *WHEN I'M NURSING A POEM*

When I'm nursing a poem,
It often wakes me in the night,
Demanding my attention.
It disturbs my sleep, insists
I change it, feed it, hold it,
Make it comfortable.
I walk it up and down the hall-way
Mumbling nonsense,
Carrying on a one-way conversation
Till something sticks.
It sucks its thumb, sighs and nods off.
I tiptoe to the nursery,
Put it down and stumble back
To bed and wonder,
Will it let me sleep till morning?

*Rowena White*

## *SMALL ONE*

Soft, sweet down by small ears, soft cheeks.
Great blue eyes, white marble, veined.
Elusive, unique smell – especially after sleep – like warm biscuits.
This is my baby, my small one, my child.

Oh God! To be *so* blest after so much pain, so much emptiness.
Years spent in the gnawing, aching void,
Spent in physical yearning for a child, for *my* child, this child.

I clutch her so tightly, making her wriggle
And tears well as I give silent, fierce thanks
For my baby.

*Chris Gothard*

## *THOUGHT-CHILD*

Today is your birthday
my thought-child
you are two years old.
You are weaned
but I am not yet weaned of you.

It is a full moon
and I have watched
how silently
and beautifully
it shines tonight.
It is your present to me
and this is mine to you.

Grieved and not forgotten
in you I find myself
and in the moon
I find you
ever present
though set
to wax and wane
in my memory
or to shine out full
as you do
tonight.

*Jackie Head*

## *AWARDS CEREMONY*

On Mother's Day the children
Amble to the chancel holding hands,
Collecting daffodils for rows of bashful Mums,
Fertile, adequate, substantiated women.
Some get two or even three or four,
Wearing them like medals on their breasts.
The rest of us look on embarrassed, rather
Out of it and unrewarded, unacclaimed
By pudgy hands and sticky kisses.
If there are some left over, maybe friends
And aunties will receive them. Honours
Second-class for those who knit the woollies,
Babysit and go home empty.
My sisters shift their eyeline, slightly shamed
By all their progeny, a little guilty
Of their wealth while we, the hungry ones, look on.

But oh, I'd rather walk away this morning free,
My bags packed ready, waiting orders
And without the daffodils.

*Rowena White*

*I AM WOMAN*

The body stands beautiful
graceful,
powerful,
"I am woman"
it shouts from every vein.

"I am woman
strong and agile.
No-one understands my thoughts.

I am woman
strong enough to stand before the mirror
naked
and ugly
Strong enough to take up arms
against the timid race
which calls itself
mankind.

I am woman
hurt and vulnerable
I can stand
in all my weaknesses
where you can hold no force.

I am woman
fat and thin
strong and weak
I can hold your ambition
in my fingernail.

My words come
from a secret well
that you can not violate.

I am woman
separate
excellent."

*Jackie Head*

## *REFLECTIONS ON THEMES AND ISSUES*

My name is Gayle Letherby. I am in my third year of a doctoral research project which explores the experience (mostly women's) of involuntary childlessness and infertility. As an involuntarily childless woman myself my interest is personal as well as academic.

The central aim of the research is to highlight the complex nature of experiences that are often simplified The study group is self-selecting and I have conducted 76 interviews with 24 women and 8 men who would define themselves as infertile and/or involuntarily childless – now or at some time in the past. As some of the issues I am looking at (for instance views on motherhood/parenthood and views on reproductive rights) are relevant to individuals who consider themselves to be voluntarily childless or who conceived and bore children without too much difficulty, I have also interviewed 15 women who would define themselves in this way. 53 women who lived too far away for me to visit or who would rather write than talk about their experiences have written to me. 51 of these define themselves as infertile or involuntarily childless, now or in the past.

The research is concerned with self-definition and identity and I am looking at this in relation to the definitions that other people (both professionals like the medical and social services professions and also relatives and friends) have. I am also considering the ways in which infertility and involuntary childlessness are portrayed by the media and how this affects people's view of the experience. The different perceptions of definitions, identities and experiences that I have encountered leads me to write 'infertility' and 'involuntary childlessness' to highlight the fact that these labels are not as self-explanatory as they at first appear. When I heard from Clare that she was putting this collection together I offered to try and draw some threads between the poems and my research findings. This is the result.

Reading the pieces in this collection reminds me of many of the themes and issues that arose in the interviews and letters which indicated that although the experiences of 'infertility' and 'involuntary childlessness' are complex, involving many differences, there are commonalities also. Many of the authors in this collection do mention the words commonly used in relation to these experiences – infertile, primary infertility, barren, childless – and in most cases go on to describe the personal feelings and thoughts associated with these labels. Often the poems describe or refer to medical investigation and treatment for 'infertility'. These remind me of many of the interviews I undertook and letters I read where the individual involved was clearly very knowledgeable about complicated medical procedures and the vocabulary they used reflected this.

The loss of the status, experience and role of motherhood is prominent in many of the poems, which again reflects my research. Reference to the implications of life without children and the attitudes of others to the childless woman (and man) are clearly an important part of the experience. So is a sense of loss and bereavement, whether focused in the case of miscarriage or an unsuccessful IVF attempt, or unfocused with reference to a child who will never be. Perhaps being involved in research or writing creatively about one's experience goes some little way to make up for the fact that this experience is generally considered taboo and there are therefore few places in which one is able to talk about it. Indeed, the people in my research and some of the poems' authors mention this. The women and men involved in my research said that it was especially difficult to talk publicly about the negative emotions that they had, for example their anger that this had happened to them and/or their jealousy of other people who had not had the same problems. Some of the poems highlight this.

All of these issues are relevant to my own personal experience, and although I don't identity totally with all the people in my research or all the authors in this collection, I find that through my own feelings and an understanding of the feelings of the people in my research group I empathise with all the writers, and indeed relate very strongly to some of the poems. Having had a miscarriage eight years ago I would echo the view that grief can be focused and unfocused as I have experienced both; yet as I have not had any infertility investigations or treatment my under-standings of the emotions this generates are second-hand. As well as being an academic and intellectual exercise, my research has also been an extremely emotional and personally challenging experience. Never before have I been able to talk at such great length to so many people about something that is so important to me. This has not always been easy, as at times it has caused me much distress both to detail my feelings and to listen to or read about the feelings of others. But I am very glad I have done it.

The individuals involved in my research appear to be a very active group. Some write creatively, whilst others write informative and/or descriptive pieces for support group magazines and hospitals. Others organise local support group meetings. I realise that this may not be representative of 'infertile' and/or 'involuntarily childless' people as a whole, as the people who come forward to be involved in research are more likely to be the ones who feel that they have something to say. However, many say that one of the reasons they want to be involved in the research is that they expect the experience to be a therapeutic one. Many also say that it is important that more people know what the experience is really like and stress that the more that is written about the subject the better, as it may help others in similar circumstances in the future. It appears to me that the authors in this collection would support this. This collection clearly articulates for me the complex nature of the experiences of 'infertility' and 'involuntary childlessness'. So I think that they are an important part of the 'telling it like it is'. I enjoyed reading them all and I am glad that I have had this opportunity to contribute to the book.

To end I would like to make clear that the above is an outline of my personal interpretations of this collection. I certainly would not claim to be an 'expert' and hope that these reflections do not distress any of the authors.

*Gayle Letherby*
School of Social Sciences, Staffordshire University